Mighty Machines

Motorcycles

by Matt Doeden

Consulting Editor: Gail Saunders-Smith, PhD

Consultant: Alex Edge, Associate Editor
MotorcycleDaily.com
Temecula, California

Capstone press

Mankato, Minnesota

Pebble Plus is published by Capstone Press,
151 Good Counsel Drive, P.O. Box 669, Mankato, Minnesota 56002.
www.capstonepress.com

1 2 3 4 5 6 11 10 09 08 07 06

Library of Congress Cataloging-in-Publication Data
Doeden, Matt.
    Motorcycles / by Matt Doeden.
    p. cm.—(Pebble plus. Mighty machines)
    Summary: "Simple text and photographs present motorcycles, their parts, and how riders use
them"—Provided by publisher.
    Includes bibliographical references and index.
    ISBN-13: 978-0-7368-6355-1 (hardcover)
    ISBN-10: 0-7368-6355-9 (hardcover)
    1. Motorcycles—Juvenile literature. I. Title. II. Series.
TL440.15.D64 2007
629.227′5—dc22   2006000506

Editorial Credits
Amber Bannerman, editor; Molly Nei, set designer; Patrick D. Dentinger, book designer;
    Jo Miller, photo researcher; Scott Thoms, photo editor

Photo Credits
Capstone Press/Karon Dubke, cover, 13
Corbis/Don Mason, 15; Michael S. Yamashita, 18–19; Nation Wong, 7; Ted Soqui, 20–21;
Daniel E. Hodges, 8–9
Motorcycle Daily, 10–11
PhotoEdit Inc./Dennis MacDonald, 17
Ron Kimball Stock, 1, 5

**Capstone Press thanks Ervin Ohotto, of St. Peter, Minnesota, for his assistance with photo shoots
    for this book**.

Note to Parents and Teachers

The Mighty Machines set supports national standards related to science, technology, and
society. This book describes and illustrates motorcycles. The images support early readers
in understanding the text. The repetition of words and phrases helps early readers learn
new words. This book also introduces early readers to subject-specific vocabulary words,
which are defined in the Glossary section. Early readers may need assistance to read some
words and to use the Table of Contents, Glossary, Read More, Internet Sites, and Index
sections of the book.

Table of Contents

What Are Motorcycles?

A motorcycle is
a two-wheeled vehicle.
It's like a bicycle
with an engine.

Parts of Motorcycles

A driver holds on to a
motorcycle's handlebars.
The driver uses handlebars
to steer the motorcycle.

The throttle and brake
are on the handlebars.
Throttles make bikes go faster.
Brakes slow them down.

brake

throttle

The engine rests

below the rider.

Big engines rumble

and roar.

engine

Riders use kickstands.

Kickstands keep

parked motorcycles

from tipping over.

kickstand

What Motorcycles Do

People drive

motorcycles everywhere.

They drive them to work,

to school, and just for fun.

Some police officers

ride motorcycles.

Motorcycles easily

get through traffic.

Some motorcycles

are built for racing.

Motocross racers

sail over jumps.

Mighty Motorcycles

People ride motorcycles
almost anywhere.
Motorcycles are
mighty machines.

Glossary

brake—a lever that helps slow down or stop a motorcycle

engine—a machine that makes the power needed to move something

handlebars—the part of a motorcycle that the rider holds on to and uses to steer

kickstand—a piece of metal that sticks out to balance a parked motorcycle

motocross—a sport in which riders race small motorcycles on dirt tracks

throttle—the grip or lever that controls how fast a motorcycle goes

traffic—vehicles that are moving on a road

Read More

Doeden, Matt. *Dirt Bikes.* Horsepower. Mankato, Minn.: Capstone Press, 2005.

Hill, Lee Sullivan. *Motorcycles.* Pull Ahead Books. Minneapolis: Lerner, 2004.

Miller, Heather. *Motorcycles.* Wheels, Wings, and Water. Chicago: Heinemann, 2003.

Internet Sites

FactHound offers a safe, fun way to find Internet sites related to this book. All of the sites on FactHound have been researched by our staff.

Here's how:

1. Visit *www.facthound.com*

2. Choose your grade level.

3. Type in this book ID **0736863559** for age-appropriate sites. You may also browse subjects by clicking on letters, or by clicking on pictures and words.

4. Click on the **Fetch It** button.

FactHound will fetch the best sites for you!

Index

Word Count: 112
Grade: 1
Early-Intervention Level: 14